MONEY MAGNET

 MONEY MAGNET

INDEX

MONEY MAGNET: LAW OF ATTRACTION

We begin...

The Law of Attraction - What Really Is and What Isn't

Objective and subjective thinking

Stop the predetermined processes that govern your life

Change your thinking process

The Right Mind about Money

Manifestation of Wealth through the Law of Attraction

Is a poor person who thinks positively about money rich?

 MONEY MAGNET

What about lotteries and windfall revenues?

Balance between the Inner Self and the External Self

Why doesn't everyone who uses the law of attraction get rich?

Conclusion

FINANCIAL VIBRATION

LET US BEGIN...

Frequency of wealth

What is financial abundance?

Frequency of Wealth and Benefits

Attracting Compatible Patterns

Understand your vibratory buzz

What is Vibrational Balance?

Changing Your Vibration

Creating what you want

 MONEY MAGNET

Learn the difference between desire and detachment

The Benefits of Planning for Financial Abundance

FINANCIAL AND WEALTHY CLAIMS. THE GREAT BOOK OF POWERFUL CLAIMS AND PHRASES FROM FINANCIAL GURUS!

Introduction

Chapter 1: What about financial and wealth claims

Chapter 2: Financial Quotes

Chapter 3: General financial statements

Chapter 4: Financial Citations in Investment

Chapter 5: Conclusion

 MONEY MAGNET

MONEY MAGNET LAW OF ATTRACTION

BOOK 1

MONEY MAGNET: LAW OF ATTRACTION

 MONEY MAGNET

We begin...

With the book "The Secret," followed by the extraordinary response you've gotten, many people are talking about the Law of Attraction. The problem is that not half of these people know what they are talking about.

The Law of Attraction is not an enchantment or a potion that will want all your problems to go away. There are things to do if you want to experience its richness in your life.

This eBook deals specifically with implementing the Law of Attraction in raising money, but in reality it is all about its

MONEY MAGNET

various applications that can help improve your life.

Free your mind from all this mess, and have a good read.

 MONEY MAGNET

The Law of Attraction - What Really Is and What Isn't

Let's start by understanding what the Law of Attraction is really about:

It's kind of amazing to see how much talk there is about the Law of Attraction and how few people really know what it is. The Law of Attraction is not a spell that is used and things start to happen that way. It's not like you say something a thousand times a day and see things happen the way you want. If the Law of Attraction were so simple, we would have already seen the world as a much better place.

People explain the Law of Attraction in several ways. The most common definition you will find will be something like this:

"If you firmly believe that something must happen, it will certainly happen."

A phrase couldn't be simpler, but you'll immediately realize that it raises more questions than answers. The question of desires is the most important. Is it just what we desire and think hard about what will happen?

Or will things also happen that we don't want if we somehow think strongly about them? Then there is also the question of the internal conflict of thoughts. Sometimes, there may be situations in which we think the

same way in both senses. For example, we may think that a job may or may not be ours. So how do we apply the Law of Attraction in such a case? Or what do we do when we are thinking strongly about something and someone else is thinking strongly about the opposite? What will happen in that case?

In order to answer all these questions, it is important to first understand what the Law of Attraction actually says.

Despite the various ways in which the Law of Attraction has been defined, we can break things down into the following four elements:

- We must know exactly what we want.

- We must begin a thought process for it, and begin to cry out to the universe to make it a reality.

- Then we must visualize a situation in which we already have what we want, and we must live in that reality.

- At the same time, we must not cling to what may happen. We just have to think about having it. There is no place for detention.

We are going to expose various aspects of the Law of Attraction and see how we can apply it in one of the most important areas of our lives.

 MONEY MAGNET

By attracting money. Can one really get rich by just thinking vivaciously about it?

We need to better understand the law and learn to apply it to get these answers.

Objective and subjective thinking

Since the Law of Attraction is so strongly based on the thought process, we must first learn what our thought processes really are.

One of the main steps in understanding the Law of Attraction to a greater extent is to understand what the word "thought" really means. Throughout the description of this law, you will find that it does not refer to thinking the way we do. We think that we exist, that we are in a particular situation, that there are certain people around us, that there are things we are with and so on.

 MONEY MAGNET

Everything we see becomes real to us, and that becomes part of our thinking.

However, this is not the kind of thought process that the Law of Attraction speaks of. This is known as objetive thinking.

But, to see the implementation of the Law of Attraction in our lives, we must first avoid the concept of objective thinking. We have to adopt a higher level of thinking, which is subjective thinking.

Why do we think our spouse is real? Because we can see it. But this is objective thinking.

With subjective thinking, things will be the other way around. We believe that our

spouse is real and that's why we see him. Now, that's subjective thinking.

Your work is not real. But because you believe so concretely that it is real, it becomes a reality for you.

Your situations are not real. However, your firm belief that they are happening makes them real for you.

This is the realm of subjective thinking. When you think subjectively, things are more or less like you are seeing a dream. When we see a dream, how do we imagine ourselves? Is our "dreamed" self the real us? No, we are the ones who are "seeing" the dream. We are only the frame of reference, the consciousness.

Whatever is happening in our dream is our perspective. This is how thinking works in the subjective world.

In this world, what we see is really just a manifestation of our thoughts. That doesn't mean those things aren't real. What that means is that these things are present in our consciousness. Just as we may be able to alter things in our dreams by applying the Law of Attraction, we may also alter things in our "real" life.

 MONEY MAGNET

Stop the predetermined processes that govern your life

We attach great importance to things that are irrelevant in our lives, to the extent that they begin to govern our existence. But there are ways to prevent them from playing with us.

To a large extent, we allow things and situations to dominate us. How often in life do we say, "This situation surpasses me! I can't do anything about it"?

We do that often. Every time we do that, we are giving up control of our lives to the

 MONEY MAGNET

situations that are governing us. We don't think a bit about the way the Law of Attraction suggests we do.

And what is that path?

Simply put, that way is to think as if we dominate the circumstances. The fact is that these circumstances are in our hands. It is up to us to create situations conducive to our development, not the other way around.

Think about this. Is there a financial problem that gets in your way? You have probably planned an effort, but you cannot do it because of a shortage of funds. So what do you do? Most people will think that this is going nowhere and they are going to save themselves. But a person who really believes subjectively will understand that the financial problem is in the frame of reference and won't worry too much about it. On the other hand, such a person will try to think that he or she could make the situation propitious.

Sound impractical? It is not really so impractical. If you start thinking seriously about having money, what are you going to do? The Law of Attraction tells you that you have to "visualize" it and behave as if you had the money.

In that case, you'll probably apply for a loan and when you do, you'll be very confident because you believe the money will be yours. Your trust will work in your favor because your potential financiers will have the impression that you have the ability to earn and repay them. They understand that you are a person of merit.

This is what believers in the Law of Attraction do. They do things leading to them through an intense thought process. But your thought process is not of this objective world. They think they are the center of everything that is happening and that they can have total control over the situations they face.

Change your thinking process

So how do you develop this kind of thinking process, in which you believe that you are the center of the universe and that everything exists in your frame of reference?

To create the subjective thinking process that the Law of Attraction demands of you, it is very important that you create the right frame of reference.

You have to be like the person who sees everything in a dream. Your perceived reality is actually the things that are happening in your frame of reference, which is just another name for your consciousness. But, you need to put a finger on this consciousness. You need to anchor it. This aspect - anchoring your conscious mind - is known as the pivot of your thought process.

When you start to turn your thinking process, the main requirement is to have a fixed point from where you can start. Normally, this fixed point is your resolution, your intention, your motive, your purpose. For example, if you really need to start a business, your resolve to do so is your axis.

The stronger you resolve to achieve it, the deeper your support will be. That's why people who have stronger resolutions are able to accomplish better things than people who don't have a very strong mentality to

accomplish something.

If you consider your desire as your axis and see everything from that perspective, everything begins to fit into place. You feel as if everything that is happening is happening as a way of getting closer to your desire. In the above case, if your desire to start a business is your axis, then you feel as if everything that is happening in your life is taking you one step closer to realizing your dreams.

This includes both positive and negative aspects. If you suddenly meet someone, you feel that somehow it will be connected to your new business, which has not yet started, but you have no apprehension in your mind about it. You also feel that the fact that you were fired from your desk job is something that will bring you closer to having your own business.

People who believe in the Law of Attraction unconditionally construct such axes in their minds. Then, their whole life focuses on this axis. This is what drives them and motivates them to get closer to their goals.

 MONEY MAGNET

The Right Mind about Money

We're applying the Law of Attraction to wealth. What is important here is the mentality we need to make this application.

What does the Law of Attraction tell us about money?

It is actually very important to point out that the Law of Attraction is not just about money. It is a very general law that can be applied to all aspects of our lives. It is a law that helps us to enrich ourselves as people, not just as financial entities. However, we are

trying to see how we can apply the Law of Attraction when it comes to attracting money.

That's why it becomes vital to know what kind of mentality you should have.

If we try to implement the Law of Attraction to this concept, we must realize that a person who is really trying to attract money must think about it all the time.

Since thoughts attract results, this is what must happen.

However, thoughts should not be objective. What are objective thoughts? Now, if you are only thinking about the amount of dollars

you will earn on a particular project, then that is objective thinking. If you can't think beyond numbers, all you do is think objectively. You are thinking how much you could earn, how much you could save, etc. These are objective thoughts and, if you applied the Law of Attraction, you would understand that these thoughts will not attract money to you.

Therefore, you need to think subjectively. Do not think about the money itself, but think about what you must do to bring you the money. Thinking about the quality of your product, for example, is a good step in this direction.

When you do that, you're really improving the sales potential of your product and therefore bringing in the money.

A person who believes in the Law of Attraction will not think, "I have to sell this product because I want to make money. Instead, such a person would think - "I must be honest in making this product and give it great quality so that I can earn money with it".

A person who believes in the Law of Attraction automatically becomes honest because he knows what it takes to get the money. They don't believe in quick fixes, they believe in long-term solutions. This should be your way of thinking about money too - Don't think about how to bring the money; think about what you must do to allow the money to reach you.

Manifestation of Wealth through the Law of Attraction

The five steps necessary to manifest wealth by applying the Law.

Here are the five things you need to do to manifest the wealth you expect through the Law of Attraction.

Believe

The first step is to root the thought of wealth in your subconscious. You have to think

 MONEY MAGNET

firmly that you will be able to achieve the great amount of wealth you are expecting.

Visualize

It is very important to really visualize wealth. You have to think that wealth is already in your bank account and now what you are going to do with it. Start thinking as if you were planning what to do with the money. You don't have it anymore, but that's not the point. The Law of Attraction says you have to be strong in your belief, and visualization is the best way to do it.

Be Thankful

Taking your belief a step forward, you must

begin to thank the universe for granting you wealth. Well, it hasn't already granted you wealth, but you don't have any defamation at all about that happening. You are damned sure that you will get the wealth and therefore being thankful is the next logical thing.

Listen to your heart

Your heart will tell you many things right now. It will tell you to do particular things. Do not repress any of these "voices. Listen to them carefully. Act on them.

You have to make sure you hear each voice because any one of them may be the only voice that opens the doors of opportunity for you.

Continue Your Actions

Never give up, never give up. Remember that stopping is a sign of weakness. You don't want the universe to understand that your belief staggers. You want it to know that you will keep up no matter what. Sooner or later, his supreme trust will bring wealth to his door.

MONEY MAGNET

Is a poor person who thinks positively about money rich?

Does only thought matter? If beggars think of horses, can they ride?

This is a question that bothers most people, especially those who hear about the Law of Attraction for the first time. After all, they think, the Law of Attraction talks about the results of the thoughts they generate, so if they were going to think strongly about something, shouldn't they realize that? In other words, if someone doesn't have a car and thinks about it, he should own the car, right?

MONEY MAGNET

Although that sounds very romantic, the problem is that the Law of Attraction doesn't work that way. It's not about thinking about getting. There are a lot of layers under here. First of all, people who think of the Law of Attraction this way don't bring one very important thing into the equation - the emphasis of effort. You don't get much without channeling your thoughts into action.

Let's understand this better with an example. Suppose you have the ambition to open a restaurant. Right now, it's just your ambition. Yes, you're thinking so hard you can try it, but that's it. Will it be your restaurant then?

The answer is quite obvious - No. The Law of Attraction is not about sitting with your bag of popcorn watching netflix and waiting for

your inner desires to manifest. You have to let the thought out of your system. You have to let it out and turn into action.

When you think strongly about something, there will be an inner voice that will tell you to act in a particular way. If you are thinking of opening a restaurant, a small voice inside you will tell you to start looking for good places.

The voice will tell you to learn the art of hotel management. The voice will also tell you to start raising funds. There are so many things that will be said by this still small voice. The important thing is that you listen to it. And you have to act accordingly.

It is only when you begin to translate these

thoughts into actions that you will be able to do something about it.

So a beggar who only thinks of a horse won't be able to do anything soon.

However, if he thinks how he should get the horse and start implementing those ideas, it is very likely that he will soon be on top.

What about lotteries and windfall revenues?

What does the Law of Attraction have to say about lotteries and all other types of wealth modes overnight?

A very common question for most people is whether they can win lotteries and have other types of luck simply by having a strong belief in them, just as the Law of Attraction would make them do. They think very strongly about winning and, therefore, why wouldn't they win? They even think about winning all the time, they buy tickets by the dozen, so the winners should be them, right?

MONEY MAGNET

The problem is that these people are on the right premise, but they are not implementing it the right way. So what's the right way? Can you use the Law of Attraction to win a lottery?

Well, for that, the first thing is to think right. You shouldn't expect a spell to come into action by bringing gold coins to your door. This is not going to happen. But you can align things to work your way.

Think positively about winning. When you do that, things start to happen automatically in a way that is beneficial to you. You probably won't become a millionaire overnight, but maybe your strong beliefs will help you earn small amounts and be content with them.

But there are ways you can go against the Law of Attraction here. If you wait too long, it's wrong. The Law of Attraction tells you to have a strong belief, but it doesn't tell you to expect a particular kind of result. Just visualize what would happen if you were a winner of a particular sum, however, do not force the universe to grant you that sum. In the same vein, if you start getting cranky if you're not earning the kind of income you think you should, you're undoing all your positive belief. Grumpy is a sign of disbelief and therefore a sign of weakness.

People who win lotteries somehow think they deserve victory. If you ask them, they will say that they visualized that they won the lottery at some point in their lives and that they imagined it so vividly that they felt

 MONEY MAGNET

it was real.

Try that. Imagine that. Visualize your result. Don't overdo it. Don't wait too long.

Things will start to line up your way. But be prepared to accept, without grudges, whatever comes your way. It will be better than what you have, if you believe in the right thing.

Balance between the Inner Self and the External Self

If you really follow the Law of Attraction, you have to work to find the right balance between your inner and outer self.

One of the most significant applications of the Law of Attraction is to balance our inner and outer selves. Our inner self is our consciousness. It is the way we think and behave. This is where the Law of Attraction begins to take effect. The Law of Attraction begins to manifest when we think and that begins within us. Our outer self is characterized by our action. The way we act and implement our thought processes is how

our external self functions.

If we are to make the best use of the Law of Attraction in our life, then it is essential that we learn to create the balance between our inner and outer selves. It is vital that we put into practice what we think. What begins as a manifestation of thought must become action.

If you would just think and sit and think about getting a new house, that is not going to happen.

Yes, if your thoughts are strong, if your belief is strong, the universe will begin to line up to make things happen. But now, you have to act. If you don't lift a finger, things won't happen. Now, you have to put your outer self into action. That's when the positive energies that have been created begin to take shape and things begin to happen.

The problem with most of us is that we use our inner self to think and believe. We say so often that we want to do one particular thing, but only a few of us actually put our outer selves into action mode.

The Law of Attraction will make things happen. But it will limit itself to aligning things in a particular way. The rest is your decision. It will give you confidence to do certain things, and that is what will influence the people around you and things will happen to you positively, but the main thing for that to happen is that you have to take the initiative and act.

 MONEY MAGNET

Why doesn't everyone who uses the law of attraction get rich?

Many people might think of the Law of Attraction. But only a few of them really start to climb the ladder of success and really get rich.

Why not all those who use the law of Attraction?

Does the attraction get rich?

If you've been following until now, you've noticed two things:

The Law of Attraction is a definite reality; everyone puts it into practice.

However, many people do not use it in the right way.

You cannot refute the force of the Law of Attraction to channel the energies of the universe in such a way that things can begin to happen favorably.

But the problem is that the Law of Attraction will only channel these things.

If we don't use the energies to accomplish what we are longing for, everything is going to be a lost cause.

 MONEY MAGNET

For example, if you only think about getting rich but do nothing actively in that sense, there is no way for you to get rich. In fact, even if you win through a lottery, you have to make the effort to buy the lottery and track the winnings.

The conclusion is clear - the Law of Attraction works, but only if you put it into practice. These are the things you must do sequentially:-

You must firmly believe that something in particular will happen. His belief must be strong and unshakable, so unshakable that nothing should distort his belief in any way.

Then you have to visualize this thing, as if it really happened to you and that you are enjoying its fruits.

The next step will be to begin to act upon your inner voice. You will hear much of your inner voice when you firmly believe in something. Acting on this is what will bring them closer to the realization of their ambitions.

So, if you are planning on getting rich through the Law of Attraction, the important thing for you is to believe and then act. Without any of them, nothing will fit in.

Conclusion

The Law of Attraction can make you rich. You must have listened to it a lot. Now you know what it takes to get there.

 MONEY MAGNET

 MONEY MAGNET

FINANCIAL VIBRATION

BOOK 2

FINANCIAL VIBRATION

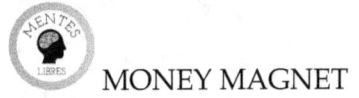 MONEY MAGNET

LET US BEGIN...

This book is designed to help you achieve financial prosperity by taking advantage of your internal resources that you may not know you have. You will learn that by shifting your vibrations and emotional frequencies from the negative to the positive, you will be able to stay focused and influence others to make success easier and with less effort.

MONEY MAGNET

Frequency of wealth

Do you think there are such things as vibrations or frequencies of wealth? Today, being prosperous or generally achieving what one wants in life seems to involve not only having the right resources, determination and skills. Possessing the right brain waves is also important; perhaps even the most important of all.

What is Wealth Frequency?

Studies suggest that meditation reduces brain waves to a lower frequency that is best for relaxing and focusing. This is known as low alpha. You can also lower your brain waves to reach the Theta frequency, which is best for lucid manifesting or dreaming. However, to tune in to the frequency of wealth, experts recommend raising brain waves.

Emotional Frequencies

In his book, Power vs. Force, David measured the frequencies of human emotions from 20 to 1,000. Hawkins suggests that at lower frequencies, people are solid or heavy while they are light and bright at higher frequencies where we get feelings of peace, love, acceptance and other positive feelings that allow us to better understand and see more clearly.

Hawkins proposes that when you are at lower frequencies, for example 20 (shame), 30

 MONEY MAGNET

(guilt), 75 (grief), 100 (fear) and 175 (pain), (pride), you are more prone to illnesses and problems because these emotions are running out and you are likely to extend more guilt, more fear, etc..., emotions that drag you and others you come in contact with.

When you are at higher frequency levels, you are able to influence others in a more positive way. To support this concept, the Global

The Princeton Consciousness Project detected a negative consciousness just before the attack on the Twin Towers on September 21, 2001. On the other hand, it detected a positive blip prior to President Barack Obama's inauguration, demonstrating that individuals are affected by the frequencies as a whole and that the earth is affected by the combined energies of individuals.

Changing thought patterns

Raising brain waves does not necessarily raise your frequency but it changes your thought patterns and you need to do this if you want to successfully diminish the effects of your ego on your decision-making and your dealings with others.

How then can you find your frequency for wealth? Well, obviously the first step is to adjust your thought patterns to one that allows you to think more objectively and clearly. The second is that you try to get up from the emotional frequencies that hold you back.

Acceptance, peace, love, goodwill, courage; all these emotions are positive and belong to the higher frequencies that allow them to influence others more positively.

According to a related study, an individual who operates at 300 is able to counter 90,000 people who operate below 200 levels, while an individual who operates at 600 (peace) is able to counter 10,000,000 people who operate below 200.

The ability to influence others is the key to finding the frequency of their wealth. This does not mean that you will not experience any failure, but as you are clear-minded, focused and in contact with a higher level of consciousness, wealth is much easier to achieve than when you are operating at the frequency levels of energy drainage.

What is financial abundance?

The life you have always dreamed of can be achieved through proper mentality and actions. If you want to be free of any financial worries, then achieve financial abundance. What it is and what it can do to your life is incredible. So, here are the things you should know about financial abundance.

Financial abundance is being in a situation where there is enough financial support to sustain your life and add a few more for your convenience.

It is far from financial burdens and worries

and there is a feeling of having enough abundance where stress and pressure do not get in the way. To achieve financial abundance, you can follow these essential factors:

What is financial abundance?

1. Learn to Strengthen Your Mind

Learn to practice a mentality full of abundance. With this, learn that money is only a material thing and should not be the source of satisfaction. Of course, who does not need money? This abundant mentality is different in such a way that it must be practiced to balance your life. Do not allow greed to overcome you. Instead, enjoy your money by saving a little and giving it away to

help. With that, your motive becomes so positive and this will eventually align with your goals. This is what is called getting positive vibrations.

2. Gain knowledge

This is not limited to the academic level. In fact, many rich people have less knowledge than the poor. This knowledge means adapting what you have learned (from school or personal experience) and finding ways to use it. This knowledge will translate into your ability, where your ability can give you financial abundance. Living a life you are passionate about counts for a life of abundance. With this, you can earn money eventually.

3. The Art of Generosity

When you want something in your life, help other people achieve their dreams too. There have been many sayings about generosity and one that is true is that we get back what we give. This does not mean that generosity means donating money. Yes, it can be done, but it doesn't all count in money, does it? So in order for you to achieve a comfortable and abundant life, create a positive environment to get what you want. Now, this vindicates the old saying: it's better to give than to receive.

4. The Way to Invest

Don't keep too much of your money. In fact, saving it doesn't necessarily mean you're creating an abundant life. Yes, saving for emergencies and unexpected expenses is important, but it shouldn't be a way to ease your financial burden. What you have to do is invest. Invest in something that will give you a significant return in a specific time period. With that, there is a great chance that you can earn more income apart from your job.

Frequency of Wealth and Benefits

The Law of Vibration

The law of vibration establishes that everything that exists in the universe is nothing more than an energy that vibrates at different frequencies. Whether physical matter or the invisible (spirit, chi, etc.), everything vibrates to a certain pulse.

Following that paradigm, everything that exists is in the continuum of energies and frequencies. One part is the frequency of wealth.

By being able to touch and resonate with that tone, you can create more of that condition in your life.

David Hawkins Calibration David Hawkins came with the calibration of human energies and emotions starting at 20-1000 frequencies. The lower frequencies are dense, states like guilt (30), hatred, sadness; love and peace are in the range of 500 to 600.

The first positive state of emotion is calibrated from 200 (value) and above. To reach the situations and the tiny components consisting of the idea of "wealth", these individual pieces must be made to resonate from the age of 200.

Calibration is not important; this is just a guide, a number we can use to calibrate up or down the spectrum of emotions or human states to achieve the effects we want.

Law of Resonance and Attraction

The law of resonance and attraction are similar but not identical ideas. Because there are different types of wealth concepts and ideas, wealth that resonates generically will attract those situations that cause financial abundance.

The law of resonance creates the distinction of whether you will attract more of one thing over another. An example is the law of resonance which differentiates whether the chair or a table can be manifested, although both are in the universal category called furniture.

Frequency Broadcasting with Deliberate Wealth

By training your mind to live on this frequency and charging it with intensity and resonance, teaching the same to everyone in your environment, i.e. employees, business partners, and even charging the physical space in which you are, you are increasing the likelihood of attracting favorable conditions to wealth.

Initially, it may take a lot of conscious effort to enter that headspace because that is not how we usually think, feel and see the world. With the passage of time, you will feel more organic and the time will come when it will become your frequency or base state.

The Midas touch

Once you become naturally resonant at this frequency, the phenomenon of the "Midas touch" begins to manifest in your life. Everything you touch seems to work effortlessly and naturally on its own, doing nothing consciously.

That is an explanation of why success begets success. It creates the impetus for success where success opens the doors for future success and so on.

 MONEY MAGNET

The metaphor of the immune system

Anyone who has achieved the highest levels of success has naturally trained to think and operate on these frequencies. Things that don't happen as planned are unnatural and are eliminated, like the immune system that kills invaders.

Diseases are negativities, and positive frequencies (for wealth) are the immune system's super-soldiers of antibodies that defend themselves automatically and naturally.

Attracting Compatible Patterns

Everything in the universe is just energy, and if you look deep enough, you will see that everything is just vibrations and that these vibratory patterns are what turn gas into gases and liquids and solids into what they are. This includes intangibles such as spirit and soul. It can be helpful to see the states of matter beginning with the ether, the spirit/soul, the gases, the liquids and finally the solids.

This does not mean that you can physically move heavy objects with your mind alone, although some claim to be able to do so through telekinesis.

That is beyond the scope of this book.

The goal of manifestation through the attraction of compatible energy patterns is to create a path of least resistance by which manifestation is possible and is a better path than the opposite of what we want.

An explanation of luck and bad luck

"If you create within yourself and without the conditions in which an event is easier to engender, something that we would consider "luck", such luck would have to be easier to manifest in an environment full of negativity and forces that say the opposite, conditions

that include "bad luck".

Due to the recent popularity of The Secret, many have misunderstood the idea of being just illusions and not taking action. Action is also energy. It is a component of force, a physical force that makes use of intangible energy and vibrations created to make things happen in the real world.

Practical aspects of energy use in the real world

There is only the attraction of ideal situations, people and events. The power of these effects generated through this channel exists in the more subtle and intangible realms, unlike physical actions that are stronger. It is not realistic to physically move an object that weighs a ton by these means. This requires mechanical energy, tools and devices such as a crane.

And how does a crane manifest itself?

You can call the company that leases large industrial machinery. You can establish contacts and make friends within the heavy machinery industry. You can visualize intensely, act as if you already have the crane. It's not just about using one on top of the other; it's about applying as many working methods as possible to achieve that goal.

On your own, I doubt that you can manifest a crane only with your mind, much less with an object that weighs a ton to levitate to another place. It's just not realistic and based on fantasy!

Creating Compatible Patterns for Wealth and

Abundance

The above example speaks of a very specific objective that can be solved by mechanical means, i.e. a crane. However, to design a general living condition with many possible variables, approach paths and results, we cannot simply reduce a problem to a single thing like a crane. And this is where hitting the law of attraction, attracts what attracts what attracts what can be useful.

By creating the right vibrations and energies within ourselves and our businesses, we are able to attract coincidences, people and resources that would not normally fall into our laps without seemingly good luck. Because we have created the right energy signatures to make these variables not only attracted but residing congruently in our space.

In short, it is about creating the right energies to magnetize assets and create a sustainable framework in which assets and resources can be maintained organically in our space or sphere of influence where these things are useful. Although they exist in the realm of intangibles, and cannot be measured with our earthly scientific devices, there is nothing to lose by taking advantage of this reserve of power available to all of us!

 MONEY MAGNET

Understand your vibratory buzz

Everything creates vibrations, subtle and perceptible only for those who seek them. Knowing and understanding vibrations, including one's own, is very important for living a prosperous and abundant life. There are two types of vibrations or energy: positive and negative. The positive energy you already know allows you to influence others and therefore do more, and the negative energy drags you down along with those around you.

Once you have learned to identify vibrations or energy as others call them, be sure to stick only to the positive ones, as this will help you elevate your own. Avoid negative vibrations that can lower or diminish theirs.

The first step you need to take so that you can benefit from the power of the vibrations that are continually released into the environment is to learn to detect and classify them. There is a proven method of doing this. Think of the vibrations you feel when a train runs on its tracks. There may not be a real train running, but you know the vibrations it produces.

Relax and open your senses to what surrounds you and you will be able to feel them. It will take time, but eventually, and with patience, you will learn to notice them. Doing meditations that erase the ordinary noises of everyday life helps. With time, you

will even be able to see them by keeping your eyes out of focus while you are meditating. You must acquire the ability to notice the vibrations if you want to benefit from their powers.

Knowing your own vibrations

The next step, after you have acquired the ability to feel and see vibrations, is to divert your attention to yourself. This will require some time for deep analysis and reflection on what your present is. You will know what they are by the attitudes you have about certain things that are of general importance to people and to yourself.

You just need to be honest with yourself.

It is important to know your vibratory buzz as it has a direct effect on how you live your life. It would be very difficult for you to achieve your goals in life if you don't know where you currently are.

Raising Your Vibrations

After identifying where you are regarding your buzzing vibrations, the next step you take is to try to raise your vibrations. There are numerous ways to accomplish this and the more you apply it, the easier it is for you to prosper and live an abundant life. One of the ways that has proven effective in raising vibrations is to maintain good health. Eating

healthier foods, drinking lots of water and avoiding toxin-laden foods raises your vibrations. Meditation, learning to relax and develop the right attitudes, focusing more on the passions of your life will also greatly help to improve your vibrations.

Generally, the happier you are, the more positive your vibrations are.

You can raise your vibrations to even higher levels by associating only with people with positive vibrations.

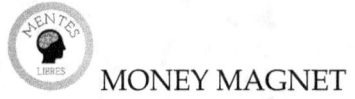

What is Vibrational Balance?

Because you're a vibrating being, you send signals that tell others who you are. Not everyone receives your signals, of course, but those whose signals are aligned with yours.

If you are sending happy signals, others who are equally happy will pick up their signals and there will be two-way communication. This is how vibratory beings communicate in a vibratory world. It is called attracting compatible patterns. This promotes harmony.

Attracting Compatible Patterns

If you recognize yourself as a vibrating being, you want to attract the signals that would benefit you. Before you can do that, you must understand your vibratory buzz. How? You turn inward. This can be done by simply calming your mind, blocking distracting noises and listening to the signals you are releasing.

Do you feel happy, sad, frustrated, depressed or contented? Your vibrations or signals will reflect whatever feeling you have, and you will receive the same vibrations from your surroundings.

Vibrational Balance

As a vibrating being, your world is governed by signals that you release and receive. In time, you will reach vibratory balance, which is characterized by the dominant signal you send and receive.

Compatibility provides stability, but is that the kind of stability you would like? For example, if you have been living under financial stress for years and this has ceased to cause you discouragement of frustration, it could only mean that your vibratory balance is in tune with this kind of life.

The only way to change a vibratory balance

that prevents you from doing more things like becoming more prosperous is to change your vibration.

Changing Your Vibrational Balance

Achieving a permanent change in vibrations is not easy. This cannot be achieved, for example, by changing clothes, showering or exercising.

Whatever good feelings you get from doing these things can alter your vibrations; but only temporarily.

To change your vibratory balance, your efforts should focus on changing the dominant signals you release. A permanent disconnection from the environment that supports your negative balance must be your priority or you will continue to return to your previous state.

There are two methods to switch from your current negative balance to one that is more empowering. The first is to change your signals in a way that allows you to repel the signals from your surroundings.

You can focus your mind and energies on your goals and this new focus that is incompatible with your current environment will slowly change that environment as you will be attracting new signals. You will be seeing and experiencing new things and eventually your physical reality will be aligned with your new vibrations.

An effective technique to prevent your environment from interfering with your efforts to change vibrations is to graphically visualize your goals for at least 20 minutes a day. Put strong emotions into it and gradually you will notice that the signals you will pick up are the ones that reinforce your vibrations.

Another approach is to move physically or socially away from your current environment. You can do this by moving to a place where the signals are different or you can stop seeing lazy and carefree friends.

Once you have changed the vibrations, your vibratory balance will change.

 MONEY MAGNET

Changing Your Vibration

Your mind is more powerful than it can really conspire with the universe.

What we say, think and feel creates an invisible vibration that transmits energy.

This energy now conspires with what we call quantum space where everything is unlimited and anyone can be given opportunities. That is why it is also considered an energetic being; not only because of physical factors, but also because it can receive and transmit energy. Do you want to be successful in life? Then learn to change your vibration.

MONEY MAGNET

It's not about what you want. What you think, feel and dream about in life can attract vibrations to it, but that doesn't necessarily mean that you will get it. These are just parts of it and what matters most is how you are pointing to the universe to get what you want. You create vibrations as you continue to exchange energy; so there will come a time when uncontrollable circumstances occur that cause the signal to be interrupted. With that, you need to harmonize everything in your life with what you want to do and repel those who stand in your way.

Therefore, if a certain situation makes you feel frustrated, angry, or unmotivated, it reflects a negative signal. Combat it by being surrounded by positive people and give energy that will make you feel good despite the circumstances.

 MONEY MAGNET

The Need to Feel Your Vibration

Stay in touch with yourself as you practice a way to create an inner peace. To cool the good vibrations, keep a calm mind and listen to your body. This can be in the form of prayer or meditation - whatever you call it is fine. You just need to eliminate any thoughts and concentrate on being quiet and at peace.

You can take a long walk on the beach or just take a vacation away from the city. For practical reasons, you can even have a good silence or time for yourself in your own room. As you stay quiet, let your emotions in. Feel anything, shout it out if you can and get it all out of your system. Feel your body's signals. There may be times when you feel a

mixture of emotions, as you may be completely sad and eventually feel comfort and peace. There are times when you are so happy and vibrant. Feel them and feel your vibration.

The Change of Vibration

Now that you are equipped to know how vibrations react to your mind, and how you can feel them, you can change your vibration toward your goal. The first thing you can do is disconnect yourself from the environment that interrupts your signal. Don't have negative thoughts or even negative people. Here's a practical tip: visualize your goal every day for 15 minutes.

Feel your emotions so strong and eventually,

you can listen to your vibrations and know how to repel the things that will block your path. The next thing you can do is change your environment. You can go out with people with strong goals like yours, change the style of your house or even change the way you dress. All of this should make you feel good and create a strong vibration.

 MONEY MAGNET

Creating what you want

At this point in this book, you should know that if you want a more rewarding life, you have to change your way of thinking, and your whole way of thinking. Here are some more tips on how you can create what you want and get what you want:

Tips & Tricks:

Tip 1: Keep your focus where it matters

Don't think about what you don't have, because if you do, you'll never have enough. This is very fundamental advice that once

taken into account, will significantly influence your life in a positive way.

Changing your focus and what you focus on will radically change your life.

If you concentrate on what you don't have, your mind and soul will continue to think you are missing something. On the other hand, when you make a regular habit of being grateful for what you DO have, you will be able to train the positive energies around you to give yourself what you want.

With this kind of mentality, you will be able to easily find solutions to common and not so common problems in your life. You will be more open to positive responses and opportunities around you, making winning

easier.

Tip 2: Define Failure Differently

One of the things that limit people from achieving great things is their fear of failure. We all feel this at a certain time in our lives. We are afraid to fail and to suffer the consequences of failure.

However, once you define failure in a more positive way, things will change drastically for you, including your perspective on failure.

Don't believe in failure. Instead, define failure as an opportunity to learn, to be better at what you just did. Without failure, we

would never be who we are, and who we are. So instead of seeing failure as something bigger than you that scares you, look at it as a ladder to your goals. Teach your mind to redefine failure, from being a negative thing that drags, to a positive and uplifting opportunity to become a more complete person.

Tip 3: You Are the Teacher of Yourself

Who's your boss? No one else should be your boss but YOU. It all depends on you what you want to happen to your life. There is no one more responsible for you than YOU. By recognizing and accepting the fact that there is no one else who can help you build your successful future, you will become more mature and inspired to do better things for yourself.

 MONEY MAGNET

Harnessing the power of the universe and making it believe what you want for yourself will be easy from now on. As you practice these tips every day, you will be more attentive to the positive things that affect the successful people around you. Then you will be able to harness this power, and make it happen for you.

MONEY MAGNET

Learn the difference between desire and detachment

Many people, armed with the best intentions and skills, still don't get what they want simply because of their misconceptions about these two things: desire and detachment.

The first thing you should know about the two is that they are not opposites to each other. However, they are intertwined because they can make the Law of Attractions work in their favor or not.

Most people think of this as a state synonymous with wanting or needing something. However, when it comes to the Law of Attractions, desire is more than that. In fact, the best way to appreciate how important desire is in a person's life is to see it as the result of having personal preferences.

What is desire?

Knowing what you don't prefer in your life can help you find out what you want in it. As such, knowing that you don't like sour food can lead you to discover that you like sweets or perhaps spicy food. These preferences can be seen as desires. In other words, you simply want to eat spicy food instead of sour dishes.

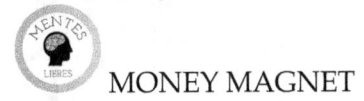

Desire is also often mistakenly considered immoral. Some people see desire as "bad" because it can lead to greed, selfishness, envy, and many other negative emotions. However, that is where they are wrong once again.

Consider the above example. Is it sinful, immoral, or wrong if you want spicy food instead of sour food?

In addition, there are many desires that one could hardly describe as erroneous or, even worse, evil. Some people just want to be healthy. Others may want to be able to help those in need.

Detachment

However, desire can be counterproductive and become its undoing when accompanied by feelings of attachment... or detachment.

- Attachment - Your desire is exceptionally strong, to the point that you feel negative emotions because of it. You feel pressured about your ability to achieve your goal. You are worried and afraid of the consequences if you don't get what you want.

- Disinterest - Desire is the only thing that worries you. You don't feel anything else. You are unable to empathize or sympathize with the feelings of others

because everything in you is completely focused on getting what you want.

Consider, for example, a student with a desire to get good grades.

Feelings of attachment can cause the student to worry endlessly about the results of tests that begin to suffer from nervous attacks and insomnia. On the other hand, a student with the same desire may use detachment as a coping mechanism. In this case, the student spends his or her time studying to the point of excluding everything else, such as eating and sleeping regularly or treating loved ones with indifference.

Desire and detachment are obviously two different things, but they can be experienced

at the same time. Ultimately, it is the non-attachment to which you must aspire if you wish your desires to be fulfilled.

The feelings of non-attachment free you from negative thoughts and emotions and at the same time motivate you to do and think better in order to achieve your goal.

 MONEY MAGNET

The Benefits of Planning for Financial Abundance

At this time, some of you may feel convinced that you know all there is to do to have the best attitude and mentality to enjoy financial abundance. That's fine, but you have to keep in mind that financial abundance also requires smart, strategic, practical and tangible actions. That's when the planning stage comes in.

6 Key Steps to Creating a Financial Abundance Plan

Planning is a process that takes time to create, complete and refine. Take your time to come up with the best plan. Changes will be more difficult and more costly to implement if you make them after the plans have been finalized.

Step 1: Increase Cash Flow

The first goal your plan should focus on is to increase your cash flow. It may not mean more profit, income or sales, but it does mean more financial flexibility. Another way to increase your cash flow is to simply reduce costs. With more cash on hand, you also give yourself better leverage to solve the problem, sudden financial crises and take advantage of opportunities to earn money.

Step 2: Investing in Health and Insurance

Health problems are one of the biggest sources of spending, so be sure to save yourself from future headaches by investing in health plans and insurance now. Speaking of insurance, it's also best to insure most - or best of all - that you have that is valuable and worth protecting. Consider investing in life insurance that also has a reasonably good payment.

Step 3: Debt Management and Elimination

It's time to stop delaying the inevitable. Today, debts are rarely repaid. Most of the time, there's no way out of them, so it's best to buckle up and find out which debts are the

most pressing and which deserve another round of negotiation with their respective creditors. Of course, this does not mean that debt is always a bad thing.

Debt can mean higher cash inflows and the possibility of allowing for infrequent investment opportunities. Just be sure to borrow only what you need or at least what you can afford.

Step 4: Increase Savings

This certainly doesn't need any further explanation. Savings are probably the safest way to safeguard your retirement and your future in general. Just keep in mind that savings can come in many forms; so choose wisely!

Step 5: Investments

Passive income is always essential in any plan to achieve financial abundance. Investments are certainly one of the most lucrative sources of passive income, but they can also be one of the most risky. Be sure to tread carefully when choosing the investment you will trust with your hard-earned money.

Step 6: Estate Planning

Finally, it's never too late to start planning what will happen to your estate if for some reason you're unable to manage it.

Writing your own will and making sure it's

airtight and legal is something you can do on your own, of course, but only if you're willing to take the time to study all the details of estate planning.

The above steps are clearly easier said than done, but they will pave the way to financial abundance if you commit to your own plan.

MONEY MAGNET

FINANCIAL AND WEALTHY CLAIMS. THE GREAT BOOK OF POWERFUL CLAIMS AND PHRASES FROM FINANCIAL GURUS!

BOOK 3

MONEY MAGNET

FINANCIAL AND WEALTHY CLAIMS. THE GREAT BOOK OF POWERFUL CLAIMS AND PHRASES FROM FINANCIAL GURUS!

 MONEY MAGNET

Introduction

Many people are looking to earn more income, increase their wealth, become debt-free and financially secure. Many individuals wonder why a few individuals are blessed with much income and others are not. Well, there are many mysteries in life, however a principle that is as old as the ages, is the Law of Attraction. Get all the information you need here.

Chapter 1: What about financial and wealth claims

What is the law of attraction? It has become an increasingly popular viral word since the wild fame of books like "The Secret" and the movie "The Secret".

However, long before "The Secret", individuals have been using positive affirmations and visualization to attract the things they desire into their lives.

The principle is quite simple. Essentially, the Law of Attraction says that whatever you are

MONEY MAGNET

thinking or feeling manifests in your life.

For example, have you ever thought about an old acquaintance you haven't talked to in a long time? You question what they're doing, and suddenly someone starts talking about them, or they appear in your life in some crazy way - you add yourself as a friend on Facebook, for example.

That's how the Law of Attraction works.

We have thousands of thoughts running through our brains every day, and the crucial thing is to fine-tune and focus those thoughts and feelings on what we want, so that what we want appears!

The reason most individuals don't earn income, or don't find income easy to earn, is because they have harmful associations and notions about income.

If you think that income makes you vicious, or that income is difficult to acquire, or that anyone who has income must have swindled someone, or that individuals who have income are selfish, then naturally, you are not going to attract prosperity into your life. If you are constantly focused on your debt, you will always be in debt.

When you begin to focus on income as a simple energy that can flow easily into your life, you will be surprised how easily it does. Affirmations can help shape your thoughts and feelings about income, so you will begin to alter your notions and get more income.

It is crucial that your income affirmations are credible to you. If you resist them, you will not be effective in attracting wealth and earning income. So if claiming an affirmation like "I'll make a million dollars this year" doesn't feel like something that's feasible, it won't show up, even when you claim it.

In this book there are income statements and income quotes that I have used in the past and in the here and now that are helping me to make income, to get income, and to have free income simply appear in my life.

It is crucial to authentically feel true gratitude for whatever you are given. Gratitude is one of the keys to happiness, and to prosperity.

The illustration, "I want to be in a satisfying relationship for life" and "I don't want to end up sad and alone" may seem like two ways of saying the same thing. They are not. To your subconscious mind, they are saying the opposite.

Your subconscious mind doesn't understand the difference between "I wish" and "I don't wish. It simply hears "fulfilling relationship for life" or "sad and lonely.

If you want to master your affirmation to produce the wealth and prosperity you desire, you have to do it right.

Although the positive affirmations come in many forms, the structure remains the same. Whatever form you choose, be as clear,

particular and precise as possible:

I am: An affirmation of who you are.

These are positive affirmations of a true state of being that lives within you. You can achieve a complete list of "I am" affirmations by making a favorable personal inventory of your attributes, strengths, talents and competencies.

- I am perfectly healthy in mind, body and spirit.
- I am a master mind and use my wisdom every day.
- I am passionate about everything I work for.

 MONEY MAGNET

I can do it: A statement of your potential.

This is a favorable expression of your power to achieve goals. It is a statement of your confidence in your power to grow, change and help yourself.

I can" statements can be designed after you have a set of goals.

- I can love my partner unconditionally.
- I can quit smoking easily.
- I can grow my business and be financially free.

I will do it: A statement of favorable change in your life.

 MONEY MAGNET

Favorable statements of what you want to happen. A prophecy of success. Affirmations of my will are made after you have established your priorities and goals. Many times the word "will" can be removed to bring the statement into the here and now.

- I will love and nurture myself better each day.
- I'll gain more confidence every day.
- I will do my visualizations every day.

 MONEY MAGNET

Chapter 2: Financial Quotes

Financial and wealth quotes can inspire you. Let's take a look at some.

Quotes

- "Women fake orgasms and men fake finances." - Suze Orman

- "If you're in the luckiest one of humanity, you owe it to the rest of humanity to think about the other 99 percent."-

Warren Buffett

- "Rule No. 1: Never lose money. Rule No. 2: Never forget Rule No. 1. - Warren Buffett

- "A man always has two reasons for what he does... a good one, and the real one." - J.P. Morgan

- "I try not to borrow, first you borrow, then you beg." - Ernest Hemingway

- "Forecasts can tell you a lot about the prognosticator; they don't tell you anything about the future." - Warren Buffett

- "People of the same trade rarely meet, even for fun, but the conversation ends in a conspiracy against the public, or in some

MONEY MAGNET

artifice to raise prices" - Adam Smith, The Wealth of Nations: An investigation into the nature and causes of the wealth of nations

- "Your actions are your only true possessions." - Allan Lokos, Patience: The art of peaceful living.

- "This story is the latest example of America's greatest political problem. We no longer have the attention span to deal with any crisis of the 21st century. We live in an immensely complex economy and are completely at the mercy of the small group of people who understand it - who, by the way, often happen to be the same people who built these wildly complex economic systems. We have to trust these people to do the right thing, but we cannot, because, well, they are scum. This is a big problem, if you think about it. Matt Taibbi, Griftopia: Bubble machines, vampire squid and the long con that's tearing America apart.

- "Our moral economy went bankrupt long before the financial one." Steve Maraboli, No Apologies: Reflections on Life and the Human Experience.

- "The basic scam in the Internet age is fairly easy to understand even for the financially illiterate. It was like banks like Goldman wrapping ribbons around watermelons, throwing them out fifteen-story windows, and opening the phones to make offers. In this game you're only a winner if you get your money out before the melon hits the sidewalk" - Matt Taibbi, Griftopia: Bubble Machines, Vampire Squid, and the Long Con that's Breaking America

MONEY MAGNET

- "Price is not just a matter of numbers. It's a satisfying sacrifice."

Toba Beta, Master of Stupidity

- "Businessmen are like sharks, not only because we are grey and a little greasy, or because our teeth follow the trail of the entrails of those we have eviscerated, but because we must advance or die."

Stanley Bing

- "No one should abandon a woman after throwing a lot of gold at her in her distress! He should love her forever! You are young, only twenty-one, and you are kind and upright and fine.

MONEY MAGNET

You will ask me how a woman can accept money from a man. Oh, God, isn't it natural to share everything with the one to whom we owe all our happiness? When one has given everything, how can one argue about a mere portion of it? Money is important only when the feeling has ceased. Isn't one destined for life? How can you foresee separation when you think someone loves you? When a man swears eternal love, how can there be separate concerns in that case?" - Honoré de Balzac, Father Goriot

- "You could still go to some industry or some university or the government and if you could persuade them that you have something at stake, then they could put the money in after cutting themselves off from almost all the profits. And, naturally, they would run the show because it was their money and all you had done was sweat and

bleed." - Clifford D. Simak, All the Traps of Earth

- "In many ways, the effect of the accident on embezzlement was more significant than on suicide. For the economist, embezzlement is the most interesting of crimes. Only among the various forms of theft does it have a time parameter. Weeks, months or years may pass between the commission of the crime and its discovery. (This is a period, by the way, in which the embezzler has his gain and the man who has been embezzled, curiously, feels no loss. There is a net increase in psychic wealth).) At any given time there is an inventory of undiscovered embezzlement in - or more precisely not in - the country's businesses and banks. This inventory - perhaps it should be called embezzlement - amounts at any given time to many millions of dollars. It also varies in size with the business cycle.

In good times people are relaxed, confident, and money is abundant. But even though money is abundant, there are always many people who need more. Under these circumstances the rate of embezzlement increases, the rate of discovery decreases, and embezzlement increases rapidly. In depression all this is reversed.

Money is watched with a narrow and suspicious eye. The man who handles it is supposed to be dishonest until he proves otherwise. Audits are pervasive and meticulous. Business morality has improved enormously. The bezzle is shrinking. John Kenneth Galbraith

- Just as the boom accelerated the rate of growth, crack greatly advanced the rate of discovery. Within days, something close to universal confidence became something close to universal suspicion. Audits were ordered. Tense or troubled behavior was noted. Most importantly, the collapse of stock values made irredeemable the position of the employee who had embezzled to play the market. He now confessed." John Kenneth Galbraith, The Great Shock of 1929

- "Personal finances are like people's personal health, crucial and tragic for the sufferer but tedious for the listener. "- Thomas Keneally, Finding Schindler: A Memory

- "The point of retirement is to live off your assets, not them"...

MONEY MAGNET

Frank Eberhart

- "The first rule of making money is not to lose it." - Steven J.

Lee, The Money Plan: Creating Personal Wealth for a Secure Future

- "Am I in debt? I'm a true American!" - From "Perfect Strangers"

- "The virtues of free enterprise can be distorted by greed and deception." - Allan Lokos, Patience: The Art of Peaceful Living

- "You won't love your investment adviser, because if she was that smart she'd be retired

by now." - Steven J. Lee, The Money Plan: Creating Personal Wealth for a Secure Future

- "You will not forget that money is only money and not character or fame." - Steven J. Lee, The Money Plan: Creating Personal Wealth for a Secure Future

- "I see dead presidents. Lincoln, Jefferson, Franklin and Washington." - Nicole Fende, How to be a financial rock star

- Many small businesses would rather face a horde of angry barbarians than deal with their cash flow situation or price a new product" - Nicole Fende, How to be a Finance Rock Star

MONEY MAGNET

- "Well, you see that girl over there, the one in that group who keeps looking at you?"... "Well, let's say I'm convinced she's wearing black panties - she looks like a girl in black panties to me - and I'm so sure that's what she's wearing, so sure of that sartorial fact, that I want to bet a million dollars. The problem is, if I'm wrong, I'm finished. So I also bet that she's wearing panties that aren't black, but any of a whole basket of colors - let's say I put nine hundred and fifty thousand dollars on that possibility: that's the rest of the market; that's the hedge. This is a crude example, all right, in every way, but listens to me. Now, if I am right, I make fifty thousand, but even if I am wrong I am going to lose fifty thousand, because I am covered. And because 95 percent of my million dollars is not in use...

I will never be called upon to prove it: the

only risk is in the spread - I can make similar bets with other people. Or I can bet on something else entirely. And best of all, I don't have to be right all the time - if I can get the color of your underwear right fifty-five percent of the time I'm going to end up very rich..." - Robert Harris, The Fear Index

- "If you owe ten pounds to the Bank of England, they put you in jail, but if you owe a million pounds, they invite you to join the Board" - Philippe Ries

- "The capital accumulated in the 18th and 19th centuries through various forms of the slave economy is still circulating," said De Jong, "continues to attract interest, to increase many times over and to continually flourish again" - W.G. Sebald

 MONEY MAGNET

Chapter 3: General financial statements

You are capable of affirming yourself to have great wealth and prosperity. Let's look at some affirmations.

Affirmations

- My financial abundance is overflowing today.

- The presence of joy in my heart releases an abundance of good in my life.

MONEY MAGNET

- I was destined to be prosperous. I have abundance to share and to save.

- Now I make a fortune doing what I love.

- Money comes easily and freely.

- Now I give and receive more freely.

- Now I attract money effortlessly.

- Now I am a powerful money magnet.

- I immediately respond in faith to the guidance of the Holy Spirit within me. I am always in the right place at the right time because my steps are ordered by the Higher Power.

- The Higher Power has given me all things that pertain to life and godliness, and I am able to possess all that the Higher Power has provided for me.

- Wealth is pouring into my life.

- I will create a home full of joy and peace.

- I am free from debt

- I'm constantly adding to my income

MONEY MAGNET

- I'm financially free

- The Higher Power is the unfailing and unlimited source of my supply. My financial income now increases as the blessings of the Higher Power take me.

- I now attract incredible opportunities to increase my wealth and my life.

- I now have worry-free financial freedom in the world!

- I thank God for my financial values.

- I can now invest my money wisely.

 MONEY MAGNET

- Now I get divine wisdom in money matters.

- I not only receive money, but I also give money.

- Now I attract money easily.

- When I give, I am given, in good measure, squeezed, shaken, and run over. (Please note that giving comes in all forms... money, a helping hand, your time for another, your encouragement, your smile. All you need is the willingness to give for that day, as directed).

- I now earn ($) a month.

MONEY MAGNET

- I have ($) at the end of this week.

- I can now give ($) per week/month to the less fortunate.

- My finances are divinely blessed.

- I am now in control of my finances.

- I am like a tree planted by rivers of water, I bear fruit in my time, my leaf does not wither, and everything I do will prosper. The grace of the Higher Power even makes my mistakes prosper.

- I attract opportunities to myself

- I'm a money magnet. I see myself as a billionaire.

- Everything I want comes to me easily and effortlessly.

- I am in the process of attracting a job that will provide financial security for me and my family.

- Wealth is flooding into my family as I speak

- I am prosperous in everything I do

- All obstacles and hindrances to my prosperity have been dissolved.

- I now have complete financial freedom to do, be and have anything I wish.

- Now I am becoming more and more prosperous every day.

- I have a continuous abundance of money flowing to me always

- I am now permanently free of debt and any kind of money problem.

- I always think positively about money.

- I have many financial opportunities.

MONEY MAGNET

- I always find a way to make a big profit.

- I am rich and prosperous.

- I have faith that I am being guided in ways that bring amazing results.

- I fill my mind with the idea of abundance, and abundance manifests in all my affairs.

- I recognize my true Source and let prosperity pour into each of my experiences.

- My partner and I take control of our finances and budget on a regular basis.

- I begin today to open myself up to greater and greater prosperity.

- My income is constantly increasing.

- I now receive my good from both expected and unexpected sources.

- I am surrounded by very smart, super effective and brilliant business people...

- Abundance surrounds me. Today I claim my share.

- My thoughts of prosperity create my prosperous world.

- My life is filled with an abundance of goods.

- With the guidance of the Higher Power, my life is full of joyful success and rich abundance.

- I release all feelings of lack and limitation. I accept with joy the blessings of joy and abundance.

- Today it is rich in opportunities and I open my heart to receive them.

- Money flows freely and abundantly in my life.

MONEY MAGNET

- Attracting money is easy.

- I am my own boss. I work when I want, where I want, and how I want, and I am paid handsomely for my efforts.

- I am a billionaire.

- Money comes to me easily and effortlessly.

- I am open and receptive to new avenues of income.

- I attract abundance without effort.

- I deserve to be rich.

MONEY MAGNET

- Wonderful things happen to me because I live with an attitude of gratitude.

- I am worthy of everything my heart desires. It is my divine heritage!

- I imagine abundance for myself and others.

- I always have more money coming in than going out.

- I allow myself to have more than I ever dreamed possible.

- I fully believe in my ability to attract money.

- I have a money mentality.

MONEY MAGNET

- Money always seems to come my way.

- I naturally attract money and material abundance.

- I trust that everything will come at the perfect time and in the perfect way.

- I surrender to my higher good.

- I invite and allow good into my life.

- I provide for myself abundantly as I go on my way.

MONEY MAGNET

- I know my value, I honor my value.

- All the money I spend enriches society and returns to me multiplied.

- My life is full of abundance.

- I am focused on achieving wealth.

- My bank account never seems to stop growing.

- I am very focused on achieving financial success.

- I am open to receive.

MONEY MAGNET

- I feel good about all the money I spend.

- My money is a source of good for me and others.

- I am financially independent and free.

- I have a large, stable, reliable and permanent financial income now.

- The Higher Power longs to bring me good!

- I am filled with the knowledge of the will of the Higher Power in all wisdom and spiritual understanding, His will is my prosperity.

- I forbid thoughts of failure and defeat to dwell in my mind.

- I am filled with the wisdom of the Higher Power, and I am led to make wise and prosperous financial decisions. The Spirit of the Higher Power guides me into all truth regarding my financial affairs.

- The Higher Power makes my thoughts agree with His will?my plans are set and successful.

- Having received the abundance of grace and the gift of righteousness, I reign as a king in life.

- I always have money.

- I attract financial abundance.

- My mind is well tuned to attract massive wealth.

Chapter 4: Financial Citations in Investment

To have good investment skills, you must have inspiration and knowledge in particular areas. Let's look at quotes from some of these particular areas.

Skills you need

- "The individual investor must consistently act as an investor and not as a speculator. - Ben Graham You is an investor, not someone who can anticipate the future. Base your conclusions on true facts and analysis rather than risky and unsafe forecasts.

- "It's not about how much money you make, but how much money you save, how much it costs you and how many generations you save it for. - Robert Kiyosaki

If you're a millionaire in the early years, but lose everything in midlife, you've made a lot of money. Grow and protect your investment portfolio by carefully diversifying it, and you'll find yourself financing many generations to come.

- "Know what you own, and know why you own it." - Peter Lynch Do your homework before you makes a decision. And once you've made a decision, be sure to reevaluate your portfolio in a timely manner. Sensible retention now may not be wise retention

 MONEY MAGNET

later.

- "Financial peace is not the acquisition of things. It's learning to live on less than you earn, so you can pay back the money and have money to invest. You can't earn until you do this." - Dave Ramsey

By being modest in your expenses, you can ensure that you will have enough for your retirement and can give back to the community as well.

- "Investing should be more like watching paint dry or watching grass grow. If you want excitement, take $800 and go to Las Vegas. - Paul Samuelson

If you feel that investing is gambling, you're doing it wrong. The work involved requires planning and patience. Still, the gains you see over time are touching!

- Funds in the investment world don't end with four-year minimums; they end with 10- or 15-year minimums. - Jim Rogers Although ten- or fifteen-year minimums are not typical, they do happen. During these depressing times, don't be shy about going around the curve and investing; you could make a fortune making a move without fear - or lose it all.

- "I'll tell you how to get rich. Close the doors. Be afraid when others are greedy. Be greedy when others are fearful." -

Warren Buffett

Be prepared to invest in a falling market and to "exit" in a rising market.

- "The stock market is full of individuals who know the price of everything, but the value of nothing." - Phillip Fisher A different testament to the fact that investing without training and research will eventually lead to regrettable investment decisions. Research is much more than just listening to public opinion.

- "In investing, what is comfortable is rarely profitable." - Robert Arnott

From time to time, you will have to step outside your comfort zone to make significant gains. Understand the limits of your comfort zone and exercise outside it in small doses. As much as you know the market, you must also know yourself. Can you handle staying in the market when everyone else is retreating? Or going out during the biggest rally of the century? There's no room for pride in this kind of self-analysis. The biggest investment scheme can become the worst if you don't have the stomach to stick with it.

- "How many millionaires do you know who have gotten rich by investing in savings accounts? I have nothing more to say." -

Robert G. Allen

While investing in savings is a safe bet, your earnings will be minimal given the

excessively low interest rates. However, don't give up on one completely. A savings account is a reliable place for an emergency fund, while a market investment is not.

- Invest in yourself. Your career is the engine of your wealth. - Paul Clitheroe

We all want wealth, but how do we get it? It starts with a successful career that builds on your talents and skills. Invest in yourself with education, books or a quality job where you can develop a quality skill set. Identify your talents and discover a way to turn them into an income-generating monster. By doing this, you can truly leverage your career on wealth.

- "Every once in a while, the market does something so stupid it takes your breath

 MONEY MAGNET

away." - Jim Cramer There are no safe bets in the investment arena; there is risk in everything. Be prepared for the ups and downs.

- "I wouldn't pay up front. I'd invest in your place and let the investments cover it. - Dave Ramsey

A perfect answer to the question: "Should I pay my ____ (fill in the blank) or invest for retirement? That said, a 30% credit card balance can become a black hole if not paid promptly. Essentially, pay off debt at high interest rates and keep debt at lower rates.

- "An investment in knowledge pays the best interest." -

 MONEY MAGNET

Benjamin Franklin

If it is a question of investment, nothing will pay more than one's schooling. Do the essential research, study and analysis before drawing conclusions about the investment.

- "The four most dangerous words for investment are: "This time it's different. - Sir John Templeton

Follow the trends and history of the market. Don't expect this particular time to be different. For example, an important key to investing in a particular stock or bond fund is its performance over five years.

- "Broad diversification is only necessary

when investors do not understand what they are doing. - Warren Buffett

Originally, diversification is crucial. Once you've got your feet wet and you're confident in your investments, you can adjust your portfolio accordingly and make bigger bets.

- "There are recessions, there are falls in the stock market. If you don't understand that's going to happen, then you're not ready, you won't do well in the markets. - Peter Lynch If you get hit by recessions or declines, you have to stay the course. Economies are cyclical and markets have shown that they will recover.

Be sure to be a part of that!

MONEY MAGNET

The investment world can be cold and difficult. However, if you research thoroughly and keep your head on straight, your chances of long-term success are convincing. Re-read these quote if you feel shaky or unsettled about investing. How are they relevant to your experience? Do you have any quotes to add?

Chapter 5: Conclusion

You can intensify your statements with one word: easily.

I'm bringing in a hundred thousand dollars a month versus I'm easily bringing in a hundred thousand dollars a month.

Notice how the word easily brings a sense of calm and intensifies the favorable emotional effect of the affirmation?

Here are some additional ways to make your affirmations more powerful:

Make sure your affirmations are bold, clear and positive.

Practice saying your affirmations for half an hour a day. Say them in your head and out loud, even if it's embarrassing. Your new vision requires courage and you can't wait for your affirmations to seem genuine - they won't seem genuine until you start believing them.

If you begin to question your claims, recognize that your unconscious mind is sending you a signal based on your conditioning - not on what you are capable of achieving.

Continue to recommit to the procedure. Each time you set a higher goal for yourself,

dedicate yourself to re-articulating that goal and imprinting it on your unconscious mind.

In addition to your affirmation, take action.

An affirmation will not cause results in your life unless you have the right plan to support that affirmation and are taking daily action according to the plan.

If your desire is to have an abundance of cash to meet your needs, practice this statement for cash: "I always have an abundance of cash to meet all my needs.

Repeat it many times, and then stop affirming. Be silent as you recognize, visualize, and feel what it is like to already

have the amount of money you want.

Feel as if it has already happened, and that all your needs are more than satisfied. While you are in that state, be open to all the ways and means by which you will attract money into your life to meet all your needs.

Choose the affirmations that seem appropriate to you, those that resonate with you, or that appeal to your emotions. It is crucial that the words feel comfortable to you and that they are in line with who you are. Feel free to produce one for your particular need by substituting other words that have special meaning for you.

Remember that affirmations take a little time, however, once you begin the procedure, you will be surprised at how quickly it happens. Initially, it feels like a lot of work without much result, but soon the momentum of the procedure begins to take over.

Inside you, there is a star that wants to express itself. All you have to do is learn how to use your conscious faculties to harness the fantastic power of that unconscious mind of yours.

Finally (read this aloud): I am achieving everything I set out to do.

SUCCESS AND PROSPERITY!!!!

 MONEY MAGNET